BENJAMIN
BANNEKER
A Man Ahead of His Time

by Ryan Frank
illustrated by Bruce Emmett

Harcourt
SCHOOL PUBLISHERS

Printed in US

ISBN 10: 0-15-351038-2
ISBN 13: 978-0-15-351038-0

Ordering Options
ISBN 10: 0-15-350602-4 (Grade 5 On-Level Collection)
ISBN 13: 978-0-15-350602-4 (Grade 5 On-Level Collection)
ISBN 10: 0-15-357963-3 (package of 5)
ISBN 13: 978-0-15-357963-9 (package of 5)

5 6 7 8 9 10   0928   12 11 10 09

Benjamin Banneker—inventor, astronomer, mathematician, farmer, and surveyor—was truly a person ahead of his time. Benjamin was born long before the Civil War was fought, long before slavery ended, long before even the Revolutionary War began. He was an African American who stood up for the rights of fellow African Americans and the equality of all people. He achieved many feats in his life. Most of all, he was a person who believed in and acted upon what he said.

Benjamin was born on November 9, 1731, in Ellicott's Mills, Maryland, close to the city of Baltimore. Although he had ancestors who had been enslaved, he was born a free man because his parents were free. His mother, Mary, had been born free. His father, Robert, had been enslaved but had been able to buy his own freedom. As most African Americans in Maryland were enslaved people at that time, Benjamin was lucky to be born free.

Even though Benjamin was born free, that did not mean that he was always treated fairly. African American people at that time, free or enslaved, were often not treated equally. They did not get to make simple choices that people today may take for granted. Benjamin's determination to end this injustice was irrepressible. He wanted to show everyone by his words and actions that African Americans were able to do everything that other people could do.

There were many obstacles that Benjamin had to face along the way. First of all, he had very little schooling. His grandmother, Molly, had taught him basic reading. Later, when a school teacher moved into the area where he lived, he was able to attend school. Sadly, Benjamin was forced to leave school before he finished so that he could help on his family's farm.

His family's farm was special. It was on land where there were a number of underground springs. Even when it was dry and rain did not fall for periods of time, the springs provided water for the farm. The Bannekers were known for having very reliable crops every year thanks to a system of irrigation that Benjamin had created. He had built a network of ditches and dams. It carried water from the springs to the crops.

Though Benjamin had been forced to leave school, he continued his studies on his own. He taught himself astronomy and surveying, a way of measuring the land so that it could be mapped. Benjamin also had a photographic memory. Once he learned something, he could remember it as though he were looking at a photograph. His curiosity for information was constant. He often tried to understand the way things worked.

When he was twenty-one, he took apart a watch to see how it worked. He used what he learned to create a clock. Benjamin carved every piece of the clock, even the gears, from wood. Once completed, his large wooden clock was reported to have worked for at least forty years. It was the first striking clock made entirely in the United States. It was also the first time-keeping device invented by an African American.

As Benjamin grew older, members of his community became aware of his talents. They wanted to help him achieve his goals. In 1772, when Benjamin was in his forties, a new family, the Ellicotts, moved to a place near the Banneker farm. The town would eventually be named after the Ellicotts.

Benjamin soon became friends with one of the Ellicotts, a man named George. George and Benjamin shared many of the same interests. George was an excellent mathematician and astronomer. The solar system had always interested Benjamin. George helped Benjamin explore his interest by lending him some astronomy books and tools.

Later in Benjamin's life, at the age of fifty-seven, he almost predicted an eclipse of the sun. An eclipse is when part of the sun is covered up by the shadow of the moon. Today scientists can accurately predict eclipses. However, in Benjamin's time, there was no exact way to predict such events.

Remarkably, Benjamin's calculations were accurate, but he missed slightly because there was something wrong in the sources he used to make his calculations. This was quite an accomplishment. It helped Benjamin to gain trust from much respected people.

In the year 1791, Benjamin received even more attention when he helped a member of the Ellicott family, Andrew, in surveying the land for a new city that would become the nation's capital. This city would become known as Washington, D.C.

Benjamin was also working on an almanac, a book with a lot of helpful information. In it, people could learn about medicine and different medical treatments. Unlike other almanacs, Benjamin's version also had weather predictions, tides, sunrise and sunset times. It also included information about the sun, moon, and stars, and even more predictions of future eclipses. Benjamin calculated all the information himself and made all the charts to help organize these facts in his almanac.

People found his almanac very reliable, and it became popular in the United States. At the same time, people as far away as Europe heard about his almanac. It became a success in France and England, too.

As Benjamin became more successful, he began to work to end slavery. One of the things he did was write a letter to Secretary of State Thomas Jefferson. Benjamin wrote that he hoped Jefferson would help make sure that the values he had set out in the Declaration of Independence were given to African Americans as well. He sent Jefferson a copy of his almanac to show what African Americans were capable of when given the chance.

Benjamin stressed that the United States would be a far better place if African Americans were freed from slavery. Then more of them would be able to learn and to create. If Benjamin was so smart and creative, why wouldn't everybody else be? This question had always puzzled him.

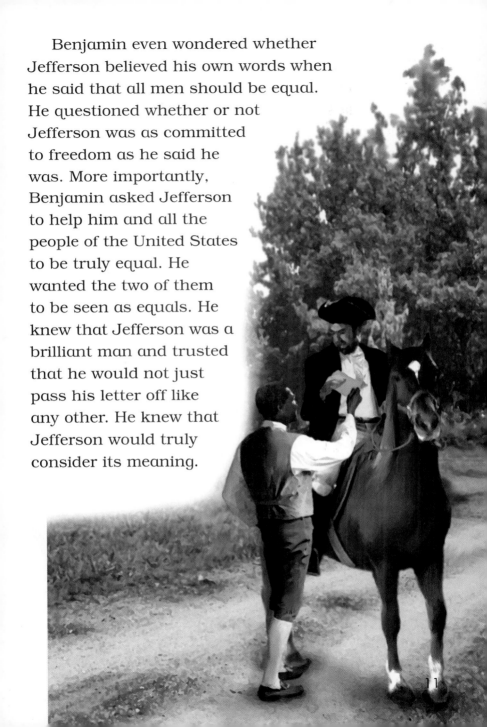

Benjamin even wondered whether Jefferson believed his own words when he said that all men should be equal. He questioned whether or not Jefferson was as committed to freedom as he said he was. More importantly, Benjamin asked Jefferson to help him and all the people of the United States to be truly equal. He wanted the two of them to be seen as equals. He knew that Jefferson was a brilliant man and trusted that he would not just pass his letter off like any other. He knew that Jefferson would truly consider its meaning.

Benjamin was right! Jefferson responded quite positively to his letter. Jefferson said that he wanted to improve the way that African Americans were treated in America. Jefferson stated that he was against slavery. He also praised Benjamin for all that he had done.

Jefferson was so impressed with Benjamin's work that Benjamin was inspired to continue. From 1792 to 1797, he published a total of six almanacs. They were sold all over the world.

Those in the publishing industry were so impressed with Benjamin's work that they asked him to write more. He soon began work on several pamphlets to let the public know about the need to end slavery.

In later years, Benjamin expanded his focus
from the rights of African Americans to the good of
all humankind. He wrote articles asking that the
United States government create a Department of
Peace. It would work to end conflicts within the
United States and abroad. His pamphlets, along
with articles from some very prestigious Americans,
were soon added to the almanac. The support of
these important people was another sign that Benjamin
had earned great respect.

Toward the end of his life, Benjamin stopped publishing his almanac. He also could not tend to his farm. He sold it to the Ellicott family under the condition that he could spend the rest of his days in the farmhouse there. Although he had already accomplished much, Benjamin continued to study and conduct experiments.

After a long and fulfilling life, Benjamin died in 1806. He will forever be remembered for his many contributions to science and the fight for equality in this country. His legacy could have easily been lost to history, but luckily archaeologists were able to excavate the site of his farm. They uncovered many artifacts from his life. Today, you can visit Benjamin Banneker's farm and learn all about his impressive life and his incredible work.

Think Critically

1. Who were some people mentioned in this book who played an important role in Benjamin's life?

2. Why did Benjamin leave school and begin working on his family's farm?

3. What words would you use to describe Benjamin?

4. What was Benjamin's main purpose for sending his almanac and letter to Thomas Jefferson?

5. What do you think was Benjamin's most important contribution to America? Explain your answer.

 **Science**

Solar Eclipse Diagram Benjamin Banneker studied eclipses. Research solar eclipses on the Internet or in other library resources. Draw a diagram of a solar eclipse. Find out when the next solar eclipse will be that is visible from where you live.

School-Home Connection Talk about Benjamin Banneker's life with someone at home. What other great people in American history does he remind you of?

Word Count: 1,403